MORE PRAISE FOR *RETHINKING COMMON CORE*

"John Jensen points out many key ideas about learning in his new book *Rethinking Common Core.* I especially liked when he mentioned that the teacher has to convey meaning and reaffirm the context. Jensen discusses concepts that help make sure genuine learning takes place."
—**James Sangiorgio**, business and paralegal law professor

"The surprisingly broad and continuing discussions about the Common Core Standards are a bit surreal, suggesting that the main issue is getting agreement on what kids should know. This book takes a very different perspective by emphasizing that getting kids to know the things described in the Common Core is a much bigger issue than just declaring what the goals might be. This refreshing view should in fact be central to all of the discussions if we are to improve our schools. John Jensen's crisp and astute writing touches on a wide range of important but under-discussed topics. This book not only recognizes that it is the lasting knowledge of students that will have long run impacts on our nation but also tries to describe answers."
—**Eric A. Hanushek**, Stanford University, author of *Endangering Prosperity: A Global View of the American School*

"Jensen's *Rethinking Common Core: The Missing Piece Sabotaging Its Success* puts teachers squarely in the camp of ensuring learning, objective knowledge acquisition, and its most critical component, retention by students of all abilities. Whether it is Common Core or learning under any other label, Jensen's model of Teaching-Writing-Boundary Key Points-Deepening for retaining crucial knowledge produces among the largest effect sizes in learning research. Moving from the self-system to the meta-cognitive system where student writing stimulates the reticular activating system (RAS) in the brain awakening the cerebral cortex, and finally to the cognitive-system, students learn to link key information to other ideas and prior

learning. The result is increased meaning, understanding, and retention. Reciting their developed knowledge to a peer, to the class, and finally before parents, students receive important affirmation for their hard work in increasing their knowledge base. Teachers will thank Jensen for his well-articulated help with a missing component of Common Core and current education."
—**Deann Nelson**, EdD, educational psychologist and education activist

"The pacing of Common Core instruction and curriculum leaves little time for retentive learning. This book will be an asset to administrators and teachers, with practical solutions that change the focus away from standards and goals that produce mediocrity, thereby enhancing the learning experience for each student within their developmental possibilities."
—**Roberta Star Schryver**, MSEd, education specialist

Rethinking Common Core

Rethinking Common Core:

The Missing Piece Sabotaging Its Success

John Jensen

ROWMAN & LITTLEFIELD
Lanham • Boulder • New York • London

Published by Rowman & Littlefield
A wholly owned subsidiary of The Rowman & Littlefield Publishing Group, Inc.
4501 Forbes Boulevard, Suite 200, Lanham, Maryland 20706
www.rowman.com

Unit A, Whitacre Mews, 26-34 Stannary Street, London SE11 4AB

Illustrations by Jessica Sanders

British Library Cataloguing in Publication Information Available

Library of Congress Cataloging-in-Publication Data Available

ISBN 978-1-4758-2066-9 (pbk.)
ISBN 978-1-4758-2067-6 (electronic)

™ The paper used in this publication meets the minimum requirements of American National Standard for Information Sciences—Permanence of Paper for Printed Library Materials, ANSI/NISO Z39.48-1992.

Printed in the United States of America

Contents

Preface ix
1 The Hole We Were In 1
2 How the Problem Arose 2
3 How Common Core Solved the Problem 4
4 The Objections to Common Core 7
5 How Standards Create a Problem 12
6 The Clue from Your Use of Paper 18
7 How the Response Addresses the Problem 22
8 Why Students Retain So Little 24
9 How a Simple Idea Can Matter 27
10 An Effective Solution 29
11 How You Can Apply the Solution 32
12 How You Can Help Students Assimilate Knowledge 37
13 How Teachers May Handle Levels of Ability 40

14 What It Means to Learn a Whole Subject 42
15 How You Can Help Students Be Creative 46
16 How This Approach Remedies the Learn and Lose System Dominating US Education 48
17 How You Can Motivate Students to Cooperate 50
18 How to Include Parents 53
19 How Students Can Perform Publicly 55
20 How to Meet Required Testing 57
21 How to Test Exactly What Students Know 59
22 How Testing Can Energize Students 62
23 How Quickly You Can Make These Changes 65
24 What We Can Expect of Common Core 66

Preface

A principle of economics informs much in life: When your horse dies, we suggest you dismount. Picture the scene. A man lies on the ground with a dead horse on him. Bending down, we say to him politely, "Sir, do you notice the dead horse lying on you?" In the range of human behavior, people can ignore even painful, distressing conditions.

Common Core attempted to address a flagrant, well-known, longstanding flaw in education and dismount from teaching practices not working well, although reforms not living up to their promotion have cast doubt on our ability to change. But limitations beckon. Knowing we cannot expect different results from the same methods, we try something else.

How Common Core will affect US education is not yet clear. Here we outline issues with it and examine a factor likely to work against its success—a failure to understand how learning becomes permanent—and from several angles discuss an avenue through it for teachers, parents, and policy makers.

John Jensen
February 2015

Preface

1

The Hole We Were In

Remember the condition of education twenty years ago that spurred the development of Common Core?

Colleges found that high school graduates needed remedial instruction before they could start classes. Businesses could not count on a high school diploma meaning anything at all. Students dropped out at alarming rates, with those of color faring worst. International comparisons rated us well below our peers in industrialized nations. Objective measures and anecdotal reports told us that students did not know what they were taught, even simple material. A high school student asks a classroom guest, "So you were in World War Eleven?" It was embarrassing.

The point was not that students learned something and it turned out wrong. Whether they were learning the right stuff was impossible to tell because they could not produce what they learned. With students punching far below their weight, stakeholders agreed only that someone else was to blame.

2

How the Problem Arose

It began in an instructional emphasis that undermined teachers' focus on academic achievement.

The disciplined learning of the early 1900s grated on many who came to regard education as too rigid and narrow. In the 1920s progressive education promoted an attractive alternative. Child development would be the new priority and would incorporate positive features such as hands-on projects, experiences, relationship skills, and social responsibility. But in a baby-and-bathwater reaction it explicitly dismissed the effort to install academic knowledge, relying instead on osmosis and presuming that it was enough to involve children in new material for a time.

It turned out, however, that exerting less deliberate effort to learn, students coasted hour by hour and learned less. Knowledge entering by osmosis exited the same way. And although many children were underperforming, by the new standards teachers could assure parents their own child was doing fine. Osmosis did not work but its assumptions persisted, affecting teachers' expectations, the content and pacing of curricula, and testing.

The result almost a century later has been a patchwork of educational attainment. Some demographics remain seriously underserved while only a few have excelled. The widespread perception, however, has been that we need to do much better and can. Students can learn more, and we can figure out what and how.

Figure 2.1. A few years ago everyone agreed education needed help. Common Core was a sincere attempt.
Jessica Sanders

3

How Common Core Solved the Problem

The designers of Common Core carved off a piece they believed they could solve, hoping it would lead to other changes. They decided to work on the 'what,' the content taught. Given that children apparently learn little from thousands of classroom hours, the thinking went, we cannot afford to devote them to just any learning. We should identify the essentials, starting in math and reading. Subject matter experts can help us prioritize, and we can homogenize learning enough to get students everywhere on the same track at the same time.

They kicked down the road an important issue. 'How' would be resolved later: "If we know what students should learn, and if we can measure whether they do, we can tell how well teachers are teaching, and work on the how with the teachers (or schools) that need it!"

Designers believed several advances could occur together—pin down the most important learning, measure students' mastery of it, and from that, determine teachers' effectiveness. While the latter assumptions have yet to be demonstrated, the beginning appeared clear: a consensus about the knowledge and skills that became the Common Core State Standards.

Proponents did not emphasize the students' part: They did not say to students, "What's important is that you meet those standards.

Get help from your parents and teachers if you need it." They didn't say this because the standards were not meant to stimulate students' aspirations but to determine a level above which adults could agree that instruction was working and below which it was not, as though this had not been clear prior to the standards. Establishing a line suggested that they believed a line would raise student achievement, but if they did not say this to students, then to whom? Who were they talking to?

The answer is "the states." The standards are a tool to help states change their system. They are to teach to the standards, run statewide tests, assess districts' progress, identify teachers' effectiveness, and respond to the results. Any child's relation to the standards serves mainly as a marker of teachers' effectiveness, and scores taken together comprise leverage.

Being able to say, "You are not working up to level . . ." enables administrators to add, ". . . so we may change your funding, terminate teachers, close the school, combine schools, or alter instruction." While state oversight may be benevolent ("Let us help you out"), officials may also assume that pressure motivates people. Feet to the fire concentrates the mind.

The energy behind this project is widely distributed across the nation, representing years of work and collaborative effort in state legislatures, education departments, and multistate agencies, and presumes a broad perspective: "We want a way to help out the lagging states; within states, the lagging districts; within districts, the lagging teachers; and within their classrooms, ultimately the lagging students. And we're arranging an objective basis for doing so."

An objective basis in fact has long been available. The NAEP, the National Assessment of Educational Progress, commonly referred to as the nation's report card, has provided solid data for a half century. The question was what to do with it. CCSS designers believed that more detailed information about higher-quality learning by more students would enhance change. This seemed important, in part because many states had accepted lenient standards for years, not fully facing their deficits. The new standards would remove that cover, so that states modifying the standards or exempting themselves would hinder collective progress.

At this writing, in early 2015, Common Core is just starting implementation and hence is a moving target. Forty-some states have adopted the standards for math and language arts, two have tested on them already, and most of the adopters are projected to begin it within a few months. While a number have scaled back their plans, enough people determined to make CCSS work may gradually produce the desired results.

Having such numbers of schools, teachers, and students answer to the same standards is a massive undertaking, particularly without a curriculum. A planner wanting a national curriculum but not seeing it as timely just now might turn to achievement standards as a first step. Teachers responding to them might realize they needed better tools and later welcome a curriculum to fill the need. Currently they rely largely on personal skills to reach the prescribed levels.

4

The Objections to Common Core

Many have faulted Common Core's advocates for not field-testing it before issuing it nationally. A sound research phase could have forestalled a host of concerns. In hindsight, a good start would have been to adopt the respected Massachusetts standards for math and English.

Majorities within samples of teachers initially backed the standards in principle, though with questions and reservations, but in the last year they have decreased their support, as have parents.

HOW DOES THE PROGRAM PLAY WITH PARENTS?

Some are dismayed that their children are taught concepts completely foreign to themselves, but numbers of them worry that low scores could affect their child's later academic opportunities.

Low scores should not have been surprising in view of the guiding rationale. The formerly indulgent messages to students, "You're doing okay," were to be replaced by an objective number. Knowing already that their child's learning was low, parents might expect the new number also to be low. Over dinner children might complain, "We used to get 90s on our tests but now we're getting 70s! What happened?"

They would realize they had been misled about their learning, were now receiving a more realistic picture, and were not being punished for the sin of receiving easygoing education in the past. Lower scores were part of the plan for change. Kentucky's gradual rollout, which included assurances for parents, sidestepped much potential opposition there, but states not so user friendly might anticipate resistance, with more parents and teachers opting out.

WHAT ARE TEACHERS' CONCERNS?

For teachers, the impact has varied according to their personal experience. While many have felt they needed more orientation and training to apply the standards, others have welcomed new methods such as ways to gain more benefit from reading. And in place of drilling children on answers they did not comprehend, teachers were to emphasize more skills and conceptual understanding, and less memorization. Instructional advances collected for Common Core could be a resource if teachers were permitted to draw on them as they wished, but left only as suggestions, the methods would be applied randomly and limit the comprehensiveness of the data.

Individual teachers have reported particular standards poorly drawn; too little emphasis here and too much there, insufficient practice for this skill, time wasted spent on that, terminology mismatched with grade levels, and required answers inappropriate. Methods over-specified can reduce teachers' options for adapting material to students' needs.

Many teachers regard the standards alone as too narrow an intervention. A curriculum (how to get there) is the missing bridge to the standards (where we want to go). Finland based its outstanding system on a comprehensive national curriculum—although with a population comparable to Minnesota's. But without a unifying curriculum, individual teachers may labor to devise afresh what someone else has already figured out.

Some standards expect less of students than teachers do already. Testing and test-prep can eat up a ton of classroom hours and interfere with instruction. With consequences pending from not meeting criteria, teachers are moved to "backmap" instruction, plan it step by step to respond to the standards. And we could consider it deterioration that teachers need to spend any time in test preparation. Students didn't learn it the first time through but now someone wants them to appear to know it.

Some teachers are appalled by the CCSS and others hate the approach. One staff member was stunned to discover students were forbidden to tell teachers the questions appearing on a mandated online test. Sequestering the material prevents teachers from targeting the test next year but also routes instruction and assessment onto independent tracks. Imagine a teacher and an administrator discussing this:

"Mr. Teacher, this test says you fail children's learning."

"But you haven't told me what I should teach instead. You say I'm below the bar but not what the bar consists of."

"You should know already. I can't tell you what to teach. We can only administer the assigned test."

"Does that seem to you a rational way to educate?"

"Look. Don't quote me on this but . . ."

It is patently unfair and violates rationality to measure people by an exacting standard without sharing its criteria. Either share the details with them and allow them to meet the standard perfectly, even though it is limited, or do not share the details and acknowledge that your measure does not fully reflect what teachers do. You cannot refuse to share the particulars of the standard and leave it vague, while still expecting them to rise to meet it. If you insist on doing this, you set them up to fail.

Standards too rigid can defy common sense. Concerned about what to take up on a given day, a teacher might think, "I want to teach a topic that would be valuable for my students and it's timely just now, but I'm required to teach one less important (or out of step) because it's on a mandated test. What do I do?"

That a teacher is even driven to ask the question illustrates how CCSS can warp education. Making the test the first concern in every situation, regardless of other factors, neutralizes the teacher's personal ability to meet the immediate needs of children that is purchased at such cost to society. Trying to make any system "teacher-proof" by assigning personal judgments to predetermined pigeonholes leads firmly downhill.

Few teachers accept that a Common Core test can accurately determine that a student's progress is unacceptable or define a teacher's instruction as ineffective. While teacher evaluations typically draw from several sources, greater weight for CCSS scores in them (as much as 40 percent) has been promoted in some states.

WHY DO STATES HAVE A PROBLEM?

State administrators and policy makers add financial and political objections. CCSS materials and teacher orientation and training can bite deeply into an education budget, so states may try to make do with less, with proportionate impact on teacher skills.

Who controls education, how they do it, and for what end is a worry. Politics, noted Hunter Thompson, is the art of controlling your environment. With the prospect of an entire district or state system unsatisfactory, politics lies in who sets the bar, how they set a passing level, and the consequences they apply. Millions in funding at stake could generate ongoing gamesmanship.

Control is bound up in the federal role. States declining to adopt the standards read into them a federal overreach to reverse generations of state responsibility. To advocates' assertions that private money developed them and that many national practices such as SAT tests are not federal concerns, opponents note recent pressure in No Child Left Behind, Race to the Top, and various funding categories.

States have often heard, "Do this and you get money. Otherwise, forget it." The president and the education secretary have urged states to adopt the standards, and the government has spent substantial money to push them. Though the plan presumes that states will administer sanctions within their own boundaries, objectors foresee the federal government increasingly tempted to pressure states with the standards and eventually develop a national curriculum. They do not expect standards-based statistics in the government's hands will assure success.

The copyrighted form of the standards has generated argument. Forbidding states to alter them may make it easier to compare one state to another but at the cost of perpetuating poorly drawn material. Some read in the standards an attack on public education by subjecting it to an unattainable measure, while others are dismayed by the profit motive among publishers.

Schools' time and resources are finite. But standards determined to be their central obligation absorb all the oxygen needed for confronting persistent problems. After attending to all the implications of Common Core, school personnel have little left to help individual children cope with the soul-sapping home-life stresses many endure daily, nor to respond to the need for better vocational preparation should we solve the prior problem, nor to implement the emerging understanding of the need for preschool (e.g., how math ability by the end of preschool predicts high school graduation).

Because the current thrust of CCSS has made standards our "hill to die on," we need to understand them better.

Figure 4.1. Students must identify what to save out of a teacher's presentation, or they will blow off the whole thing.

Jessica Sanders

5

How Standards Create a Problem

Standards surface in the argument over accountability and testing as they define acceptable achievement. But other facets of the CCSS, such as new methods, may also influence outcomes, and teachers always have the presumptive goal of conveying to children what they do not know. If progress occurs, we may want to know which aspects generated it. Among those the CCSS introduces, we particularly want to know how measurable standards figure in, and why top-down initiatives may not succeed.

An apex outcome can drive out everything else. Organizations can declare a dominant standard, the one others answer to. Call it "the apex outcome" they want so much they sacrifice other values to get it. This is military-type thinking, a focus on an objective when only one matters. If we send a lander to Mars, every decision serves a landing on Mars. If a corporation determines to maximize shareholder profit, every corporate act supports that mandate and reroutes other constraints.

While subscribing to many other values in their abstract form, schools can make test scores the apex outcome rather than the substance of learning behind them, or their effect on students contributing them. Obsession with scores led to the cheating scandal that rocked the Atlanta school system. Administrators believed achievement must look a certain way, a guess about national values probably not far off the mark.

The design of Common Core assumes that reconfiguring content and testing, retraining or replacing teachers, and pressing districts will cause change. But in place of these indirect influences, rapid change in learning is more likely from changing what students do, which occurs as teachers request it and students comply. Because teacher directions are the main force guiding students' hourly actions, for rapid results we rethink what teachers ask for. If our apex outcome is to get students to learn permanently, we open to means other than standards. We cannot immerse ourselves in a single factor that consumes everything else we want.

STANDARDS MAY HAVE A SIGNIFICANT IMPACT ON INDIVIDUAL STUDENTS

Standards can depress or energize. They are a way of tracking progress. As we set them for ourselves, they can energize us so that we are pleased to reach one after another as we advance. Standards others set for us can also inspire us. Great leaders pose high standards and help people attain them. A successful businessman declared, "Never underestimate people's ability to achieve your dreams." He understood what it took to move others to work together willingly.

Standards can pose a clash of values. Comparing what we are to what we should be, we may be surprised to discover ourselves below par. Leaders, in fact, may let us know they see us that way. When they give up motivating us with positive standards and resort to threat and control, they may maneuver us onto the path they want by making the alternative troublesome to us.

But standards laid upon people as a burden work differently than those offered as ideals. Pressure is a put-down. When people recognize it, their ability to sacrifice for a worthy goal diminishes. A leader telling them, "You have no ideals I can appeal to," means they must fight off such an influence just to do their job with a good heart. At a primitive level, human behavior can be directed by negative consequences. Strike them as they turn left and they will turn right instead, but we cannot prepare children for a free society in a repressive manner. They learn values from their experience of them, and we may ignore how distant it can be from the values we say we want.

A clue about this surfaced in the 1960s shortly after Sputnik went into Earth orbit, and many wondered if we might learn a lesson from Soviet education. Royce Van Norman wrote then in *Phi Delta Kappan*:

> Is it not ironic that in a planned society of controlled workers given compulsory assignments, where religious expression is suppressed, the press controlled, and all media of communication censored, where a puppet government is encouraged but denied any real authority, where great attention is given to efficiency and character reports, and attendance at cultural assemblies is mandatory, where it is avowed that all will be administered to each according to his needs and performance required from each according to his abilities, and where those who flee are tracked down, returned, and punished for trying to escape—in short in the milieu of the typical large American secondary school—we attempt to teach 'the democratic system'?[1]

Although education has changed somewhat in a half century, the description remains too recognizable and the hint still timely:

Align children's experience with what you want them to learn.

Standards can aid achievement if students perceive them as enhancing. While we may say "This is for your own good" as we jerk them about minute by minute, they must feel it matters to them and buy into its aspirations. Below, we explain how. But a test whose message is "You don't measure up" depresses them unless they want to measure up. So as districts hear they must teach better or will be penalized financially, embarrassed publicly, or dismembered administratively, we should not expect this to generate much student achievement.

STANDARDS CAN HAVE REVERSE EFFECTS

Misplaced standards may distract students from what they can actually do. Standards should benefit students, but might do so in different ways. Some are trade-offs—an early, small but negative impact in return for a later, large but positive one, such as when early (unpleasant) discipline leads to later (gratifying) mastery. But noticing that we affect students negatively, we need to trace cause and effect carefully.

The data unit of a district's achievement record is a single student's score on a subject-matter test.

If the student is above the cutoff, the test tells him, "You meet expectations," implying "You can ease up now. You've arrived." He is pleased and eases up, as does another who meets the standard: "Okay here. No cause for alarm. Just keep going." The line separating acceptable from unacceptable does not help either.

But what about a third student falling well below the line? From formative testing we expected he would, but we already know how to help him by combining feedback with support: "Hey, great news! We've figured out the block that holds you back."

How does the CCSS add value? What gain is there in telling him, "Hey, Bud. You are way, way below standards!"?

There is none for the student. For him or her, information arriving that way is at best meaningless or at worst discouraging. If the eventual point of our effort is student achievement, how do we come off programming great resources into controlling for something that, on the face of it, is neutral to students or poised to damage them?

A misjudgment at work here arises from a cultural misconception that appears to have influenced the development of Common Core. It is the belief that "high" means better, regardless of conditions making it counterproductive.

Years back, people assumed that students were not learning because we demanded little of them. Demanding little was translated into "We had low standards," and demanding more meant "high" standards. But "more" and "high" can work in reverse unless we know what we are doing. A middle school enlists a retired National Football League coach to lead its football team, but the entire team quits to protest his "rigorous" standards.

We can insist on whatever we want with absolutely no effect on what we get. Say we have a middle school high jumper who can clear four feet. Everyone else on his team does five, so we demand five from him. We send him out on the track, he misses badly, and is embarrassed. Poor kid just couldn't cut it, right?

By no means. We set him up to fail. We humiliate him by subjecting him to an unworkable standard. For him, the bar should have been at four feet one inch. We set the bar for each at their own level, not higher, not lower, and certainly not at the average height for all the participants at the meet.

Standards can obscure the actual focus of effort, drawing attention to a particular point on the continuum of progress regardless of whether students' capability leads it or trails it and even if it is irrelevant to the changes we want.

Students advance by exerting effort at the level they now occupy, effort we can vary in minutes. Our target for each should be what they can reasonably respond to. If we preoccupy ourselves with issues that appear larger, we are not likely to achieve our purpose. Big stuff has to translate into small stuff. Each student must still progress step by small step from where they are, just as before Common Core.

WE APPRECIATE A TRUE HIGH STANDARD BETTER AS WE APPLY IT TO OURSELVES

A true high standard is personal and internal. For us adults, a standard must first be possible. If we can't do it at all, it's not high but only out of place, and we automatically dismiss such aims. A true high is within our power when we draw on ourselves differently—perhaps with more focus, work, thought, risk, or persistence—but it applies to the leading edge of a relatively small gap.

The low side of the gap is what we have already done or can do easily. The high edge is a greater effort we can still carry out but only on one task at a time. Completing an assignment and taking up the next, we are again at the low edge of the opening in front of us and proceed into it with new energy. We constantly must regenerate fresh motivation and restore our command over our capabilities.

Students have a similar margin between what they do easily (or have completed) and their next task requiring new effort. They progress as they cross it. We define the effort within their power (often distant from group norms), get them to do it, and then continue in that direction.

NOTES

1. Royce Van Norman, "School Administration: Thoughts on Organization and Purpose," *Phi Delta Kappan*, 47(1966): 315–16.

6

The Clue from Your Use of Paper

We humans tend to keep anything in which we invest energy. Even if we don't foresee using it soon, our effort defines its value to us, telling us not to discard it. We might view today's disposable culture as a historical aberration. Because possessions inform us of aspects of the world we have brought under our control, we are natural accumulators and need to be trained to throw away objects that are still useful.

Students intuitively want to retain what they care about, and show it by saving its hard copy—think of their cache of video games, music CDs, and sports paraphernalia. Learning is no different. If your class studies a text and at the end of school could keep it if they wished, would they do so? If you generate their interest, many would.

Years ago I conducted a small school in my home for middle and high school students having difficulty in the public system. One day I met with a junior seeking admission.

When I asked her what she had been working on in English, she drew a sheaf of papers an inch thick from her pack and dropped it in my wastebasket.

"This is English," she said.

"Wait a minute," I protested. "There must be something worth saving." Students saving whatever they put effort into learning was a priority in my school.

"No," she answered matter-of-factly, "there isn't."

Later I retrieved the papers from the wastebasket and went through them a page at a time. She was right. From months of work by her and her teachers, nothing was worth saving. How could this be?

Several possibilities point toward students giving up any attachment to the learning contained in their papers.

An optimistic inference could be that the material enabled them to gain a permanent skill. Once achieving their purpose, the pages no longer aided students' practice and could be safely discarded. This probably applies to very few courses and a scant handful of pupils.

A second possibility is that the subject itself—English as literature, English as skill in speaking and writing—contained nothing worth saving or improving, that whatever students picked up already was enough. If the instructional goal was only familiarity

Figure 6.1. Students discard their learning when their school does not expect them to keep it.

Jessica Sanders

anyway, mastery of specific material was not the point. The current design of instruction probably leaves many students and teachers with that belief.

Third, the papers might have contained nothing students personally valued. This would be more likely if the content was impersonal, if they did not produce it nor connect it to their lives, and if it was poorly designed to begin with. This should not apply to the study of English, but students might see it that way.

A fourth angle is that by the end of the course, students developed no permanent skill from using the papers, but instruction did not commit them to continued learning. The papers did not offer a means for them to progress further, and the system gave up trying to motivate them.

A modest study could find out which of these factors or others might explain students' habit of discarding their hard copy, but I would check the last three—skill not sought, no personal value, and the system giving up on them.

Will Common Core be any different? If the materials I have seen so far represent the whole, it will produce tons of paper not worth saving, containing nothing children will want to keep and return to. They will throw it away with the same indifference they already dismiss what they learn.

Proponents of learning by technology, on the other hand, believe they solve several problems by discarding paper altogether and placing each child before a computer that supplies and tracks their every step. While students may gain information this way, they may miss out on important qualities. Value lies not just in acquiring data but in intangibles such as enjoyment of learning, welcoming thought about its result, and connecting to others over it.

Knowledge accrues such qualities by how it is taught. If students feel isolated in their science classroom, science as a subject feels isolating. If students are treated impersonally in English class, English feels impersonal, but an engaged social studies classroom makes the subject seem engaging. Teachers and students color a subject by how they exchange its ideas. Students treasure learning laden with personal experience, connection to peers, and good feelings.

Technology slices away the unprogrammable parts that are conveyed by people. No computer key supplies the enthusiasm that helps you carry knowledge with you, savor the good parts, discipline yourself to work harder, share your best ideas courageously, and return to a rich reflection on more knowledge. Information stripped of humanity conveys fewer of the values that should illumine a child's social existence.

But in the history of humankind a new invention stands out whose potential to aid education has not been plumbed—print. A book I ran across recently was a history of science and technology designed for upper grade school. It was a lucid, engaging narrative about the development of scientific thought, replete with illustrations and personal profiles, and on practically every page contained ideas I did not know. Probably fewer than one in a hundred adults would be familiar with its contents—a book designed for grade school.

We could supply every child in the third grade with their personal copy of it. If schools were then to teach it, expand on it, and enrich it for three to five years, 99 percent of students could easily graduate grade school with more knowledge of science than they now carry away. We spend billions to teach them answers to test questions they will quickly forget when we could spend far less to leave them with far more. For ourselves, we keep a hard copy of anything we are serious about learning, but retrieve from children the books that might interest and benefit them.

Few practices are more likely to encourage lifelong learning than enabling students to experience the enjoyment of learning from their own books, but we have some convincing to do. A mother reports helping her high school son choose a birthday present for a friend.

"You could buy him a book," she offers gently.

"No," her son replies, "he has a book."

7

How the Response Addresses the Problem

The reader might notice a mismatch between the problem explained in chapters 1 and 2, and the solution offered by the CCSS; like the problem is throwing a football but the response is catching a baseball. Our problem was that whatever students learned was not staying with them. Curricula may have offered great content, but students did not hold onto it. Retaining it was their problem.

But in a shift of focus, the response was to say, "We need to teach something different. We are not teaching them even doubtfully helpful material so they retain it now, but we are sure that if they have better content, they will absorb it."

The data eventually will reveal if learning different material is the answer, but we should not presume so. The design of US education that structures Common Core ignores a principle about how the mind accumulates knowledge:

Dismissing knowledge reduces its retention.

Just expecting to have to produce certain knowledge later markedly increases memory of it. Telling yourself you don't care if you remember it, you release it to evaporate quickly. Applying this attitude to a course, you make its content dissolve faster.

For yourself, let's say you have to sit through a course, are told you will be tested on it and that that will be the end of it—you will never have to return to it again—what do you do? Do you dive into it eagerly, saying, "Oh, boy! A way to use up my time! Just what I was looking for"? Or do you say, "Arrrghhh. To get through it, I'll do what I have to so I can move on to the good parts of my life"?

Odds are you groan, get through it, and afterward drop the material in a drawer or wastebasket. You dismiss it.

Students are worse off than you are because they face an added obstacle. We even tell them we do not require of them permanent learning. We do this by design, coast to coast, and structure their time accordingly. Consider how it happens.

Figure 7.1. Writing out their lesson helps students define it, claim it, and learn it. Knowing specifically what to master increases their confidence.

Jessica Sanders

8

Why Students Retain So Little

As we ponder improvements to our education system, we wonder what better ones, like Singapore's or Finland's, do differently. But their methods alone may not fully convey a crucial attitude. In top plans, teachers believe that students must and will retain their learning, and they arrange instruction to accomplish that. The US system instead tells students, "We don't care if you keep it or not." Students keep little because we show them in several ways that that's what we expect.

- You end a course and test your students, but what happens after? When a course ends, students drop it.
- You never ask them to keep the knowledge permanently.
- They have no comprehensive hard copy they personally own and account for, so they cannot correct errors.
- Their learning is piecemeal rather than comprehensive.
- The tests they face were largely recognition-based—guessing among possible answers.
- Pretest reviews simplify test taking.
- Sustained personal interest has little place because "we have to go on."
- Tests are scheduled, encouraging cramming.

- The word "final" heads their last test, telling them, "This is the end."
- Learning and nonlearning alike are dismissed.

To appreciate how these conditions affect students, notice how they affect you. Even courses for adults follow the pattern I refer to as the Learn and Lose System. Recall a required but easy course you took, and how your students' reactions today match your own back then.

1. The instructor explained the material and later asked questions, expecting you to grasp the material briefly and lay it aside. It never occurred to you to turn it into ongoing knowledge, and when your instructor said as much, you thought "Yay!" You knew no one would ask continued effort of you. Bare familiarity was your intent. No one ever brought up permanent retention of a body of knowledge.
2. Structurally the course started on one day and ended on another. Afterward you and your peers knew you would no longer be responsible for it. Since no pressure would follow you, you were relieved that you need exert no further effort. The course satisfied a checkpoint.
3. A few handouts were sufficient for the course, and no one asked you to write out its content. No comprehensive hard copy meant that any vagueness in the presentation remained in your understanding. You couldn't look up and restore forgotten material. You discarded the hard copy of your assignments as soon as the teacher recorded their score, and did not integrate them into course material. Without written details, a course easily reverts to temporary, vague, disconnected responses.
4. Instructors proceeded through the material piece by piece. Although they may have grasped the subject thoroughly, they did not expect you to do so and instead asked you to respond to questions piecemeal. As long as you could answer them, it didn't matter if you integrated them.
5. The tests in your course were recognition-based, true-false, or multiple choice. A good test taker could answer a quarter of the questions correctly with little study, and answers from the barest clue scored the same as knowing a point thoroughly.

6. Your personal interest in the subject was irrelevant because the curriculum prescribed the pace of learning. You had no incentive to pursue it on your own, integrate it at a deeper level, or expand your horizons. You were given a quantity of knowledge to swallow, did so, and expected to be free of further bother.
7. Pretest reviews sifted through likely test questions, so that all other time you spent on the course was just familiarizing. Answering the review questions got you through. The teacher wanted you to look as though your score represented ongoing knowledge.
8. The instructor scheduled the final exam at a specific hour so that everyone counted on cramming unless the test was open book, reducing even minimal prior study. With cramming, students appear to know more than they actually do because they quickly forget what they learn.
9. The word "final," as in final exam, means "the last time you will be accountable for this knowledge," unmistakably informing students: "You can drop it after this, you are done with it, and welcome to forget it." "Final" declares an end both to effort and interest. The school tells students to move on.
10. Completing a test, some students do well and others do not. Thorough instruction would reinforce correct answers but especially work with the incorrect to ensure students carry forward accurate knowledge. Yet both are dismissed together. A grade of C means that even knowledge held temporarily for the test was mediocre to begin with, and mediocre, temporary knowledge dissipates quickly. Both A and C students drop their learning.

These ten conditions direct students to discard their learning. Should they wish actually to keep it alive in their mind, they must work against the Learn and Lose System. Their school tells them daily that the knowledge they labored to learn before is not important any longer—except during the time window of a high-stakes test when they must appear to know it.

9

How a Simple Idea Can Matter

Progress resumes by reversing the factors above, but they need an organizing idea—why do this? Why do that? Proposing even the possibility of a solution, however, may raise eyebrows. Many assume there could not be one, that education is too complex, too personal, or too political; or that too much is known already for any simple thing to matter now.

But think about it. For centuries people died under medical care and doctors did not know why. The first ones to understand what their hand washing meant must have been shocked. Imagine a conscientious surgeon facing himself in a mirror and admitting, "I've been killing people all these years by infecting them with dirty hands." Hand washing seemed too simple to make a difference.

When the Russians launched Sputnik into Earth's orbit, the public was awed. Eventually people understood that when an object's rate of fall away from the Earth matches the pull of gravity toward it, it remains in orbit—a simple principle with historic consequences. Gravity and velocity were known from forever ago, but few connected them.

Twenty years ago, finding student achievement as simple as gravity, I titled my first manual for teachers *Easy Learning*, and carried it to schools that allowed me ten minutes at a faculty meeting. A middle school teacher glanced at the title and exclaimed to a colleague,

"Nothing is easy." Many assume that if learning is easy for students, there must be something wrong with it, that easy means we fail.

But if we can do it at all, it's easy. The word describes principles that bring results reliably and efficiently even though strenuously—like Archimedes declaring that with a fulcrum, lever, and place to stand, he could move the earth. With the right ingredients, it's easy. It's easy that skill at anything arises from practice plus insight. This has been known for generations yet only sporadically applied to school performance.

Or consider time use. Is it that hard to distinguish critical uses of time in the classroom from marginal, and to spend more on the first and less on the second? If we think about it, it's easy to connect our actions to the results we want.

Figure 9.1. Knowledge students learn from each other matters more to them and becomes the content of their relationships.

Jessica Sanders

10

An Effective Solution

As a teacher you exhibit a solution every day although your students may not. For yourself you put to work a familiar axiom that begins with "To learn a subject . . ." That's what we want students to do, learn a subject, not just piecemeal answers. The next two words explain how: to learn a subject, teach it. That is to say, by teaching it you learn it. Something you do in teaching it causes you to learn it. And what is that?

First separate input and output. With input you gather information. Like your students, you listen, read, take notes, do assignments, and have the usual tests. Input is not a distinguishing feature but output is: how you express what you absorb.

1. The main difference between you and your students is that in teaching you talk a lot about the subject. Compare your time gathering information to your time explaining it, your relative amounts of input and output. A few minutes on the Internet or reviewing notes (input) prepare you for hours of instruction (output). You may have expressed twenty times over the material you learned in an hour of college study. Teaching sections of the same course, you might have repeated the material several times on one day, thoroughly assimilating that college hour into your mental field. For every hour you read

currently, you may talk five to ten hours about it over weeks and months, shifting from one facet to another and adapting your comments to your receivers because the field lies open in your mind.

And while you may talk a lot about your subject, your students probably do not. To appreciate this, visit a class. Pick any subject, grade, or instructor. Even good teachers are likely to follow this pattern. Randomly choose a student—those seated in back may need attention most. Pull out your second-denominated kitchen timer and measure exactly how much time your selected student expresses his learning during that hour. The teacher has been coming at everyone with input, input, input. The spotlight circles the room and may even pass him by so that he says nothing at all while you are there. But if by chance it settles on him, he gets to say something. How much time is he allowed?

Odds-on it will be less than a minute per hour, and even then with only a sentence responding to the teacher's question or a word filling a blank in the teacher's sentence, so it helps his learning very little. About 80 percent of student comments are in thirty words or less. Teachers who provide inclusive subject-matter interaction, on the other hand, typically see gains in learning.

2. The second difference between you and your students is you enable someone else to understand. You note your own array of knowledge, grasp what the other (person or class) understands, and fill in between the two fields. You don't just supply details like answering test questions. Rather you convey meaning, beginning from how another apprehends the material, or may build a fresh field in students' minds.

   Repeatedly reaffirming the context ("Where does this belong?") helps you move to any part of your knowledge ever more flexibly. Explaining is putting this process into words. You link memory of facts with reasoning that connects them using understandable words. Thinking is explaining something to yourself.

3. You also embody ideas, connecting them to words, gestures, and physical actions, and infusing them with emotion. Your interest and enthusiasm color your ideas to make them more attractive to you and your students.

Figure 10.1. By explaining a subject, students absorb it better and teach each other.

Jessica Sanders

11

How You Can Apply the Solution

Besides gathering information as they do already (input), students also need to express it like you do (output): Talk more, enable others to understand, and infuse knowledge with feelings. Beyond piggybacking on others' remarks, like you they must call up the field itself from their own mental stores, organize it so it makes sense to them, and help someone else understand it.

But how could your classroom accommodate this? You already have too little time, so how could you shoehorn in so much student talk?

Remember that you and the whole class together are not the only listener. Instead students build skills and relationships if you pair them up (or arrange small groups), and teach them to listen to each other.

From third grade on, students who by now are reading to learn can do this, although the principles apply as well to younger children—a need that has some urgency. Enormous numbers of them enter school with a word deficit, just not hearing and saying enough of them at home. If you want them to learn words fast and remedy the deficit, arrange for all of them to talk about their learning all day. If you have not thought about how to accomplish this (parents should have done it, right?), go to *Effective Classroom Turnaround: Practice Makes Permanent*, Rowman & Littlefield (2012), chapter 5, section 34, Primary Grades. Outlined there is a format enabling first graders and kindergarteners, even the reticent, to talk about what they learn.

We can arrange instruction in four steps:

1. First is that students understand the lesson. To help you with this, you have curricular materials, direct instruction, individual tutoring, and peer help. Track carefully how every child forms their initial grasp. Subsequent steps become possible only after that. Consider not explaining anything to a student yourself that another student can explain. You have a whole class of aspiring teachers to put to work.

   Many teachers end instruction once they believe students understand a lesson. They are not committed to all students' permanent retention of it.

   Come again? Not committed to students' permanent retention of their learning? You take students on to the next lesson once they understand this one, and that means you are not committed to its retention? Maybe you protest, "Me!? Of course I'm committed to . . ."

   Let me wave a caution flag. We can explain this point step by step, but if there is a deficit in your approach, you probably don't want to hear it, just like the rest of us. None of us like acknowledging a flaw in our actions.

   So let's guess. First you present some material, but, hey, Andrew is drawing a picture for his girlfriend, Carl is half asleep, Jennifer is talking to Sophia about her hair, but you persevere. You corral the distracted, ask a few prompting questions, explain some more, and finally either run out of time or declare, "They get it!" They all understand the point you make although you know their attention ranges from dim to good.

   What happens next? Do you go on to add more material or do you set them all on track to master this much? You may think, "I've got to go on. We'll come back to this later and review it," or "I'll give an assignment about it." But in a sense the question then will be the same you face now. How will Andrew, Jennifer, Carl, and Sophia master this material that they grasped dimly to start with? If you have no strategy, they are sure to remain at the bottom of your curve. How will you get all of them up to speed, the slower included? The next steps explain.

2. Then students put in writing what you tell them plus what they extract from materials or reading. There are several reasons for this.

   Students obviously learn to write only by doing so. Writing also to summarize what they learn serves two needs. They write to practice writing and to save their learning. By doing both together, you demonstrate to them how word choice, spelling, punctuation, and grammar help them record and transmit their thinking clearly.

   From its use in mathematics, we can extrapolate how writing connects up ideas in all subjects. Students solve a math problem by writing each step as they do it. Beginners would be dismayed if they had to apply only mentally all twelve steps of long division without writing them, for example, to say nothing of more complex processes. But all subjects have comparable, though less exacting, relationships between the whole and the steps or parts comprising it. Writing them down makes them clear and learnable.

   For many students, the physical act of writing connects them to the details the material requires. They focus differently on what they write than on what they hear, and are more likely to own it. You can practically see them carve a word into their brain as they write it in context. Sir Francis Bacon summed up the point: "Reading makes a full man, writing an exact man, and conference [conversation] a ready man." Because students read and write little, among those passing through our system few come out full, few exact, but many ready—ready with vague, ill-defined ideas. Without a written account of it, knowledge loses its edges and is more easily forgotten.

   Writing is particularly important for students of lower ability. Often their study habits, ability to focus, or prior academic experience condition them to believe they simply will not get the whole thing, whatever it is today. Writing down their learning as it arrives per teacher's instruction solves this problem by distinguishing clearly what they are responsible for, and puts it in a form they can use to learn it. Of the four steps noted here, this second one signals your personal resolve to guarantee their success by creating the tool they need for practicing their knowledge.

For students who know keyboarding, ask them to summarize each day's learning and steadily assemble their year's knowledge into a comprehensive resource. The Common Core aim of tests with more essay and fewer multiple-choice questions is positive, but the need for writing is far greater than occasional appearance in standardized tests. And a limitation on its use there is that in order to grade essay questions mechanically, designers must dumb down the writing so that an algorithm rewards a given formula.

3. A boundary helps students carry forward, practice, and master material. You do not ask them to retain your fifteen-minute presentation verbatim (or their reading, assignment, class discussion, or project). Particular items mark your objectives for the lesson.

   Perhaps you present a question and five key points in answer. The class together might select the phrases best describing the points as you write them on the board for all to copy. Maybe they enjoyed a class discussion about a poem or paragraph. To save its benefits, have students write them down so they all have a cumulative, succinct, understood, socially affirmed hard copy of what they will turn into permanent, lifetime knowledge.

4. The last step is deepening this defined material by expressing it. Telling it to each other, students master material they otherwise would retain poorly. The hammer driving the nail is their narrative about it that you set up by partner practice. They explain the answer to today's question and all others from the beginning of the course, deepening understanding and retention together.

   Presuming conflict between those two processes is flawed psychology. While it should make no sense to us to drive students to recall data that makes no sense to them, Common Core's aim to increase understanding by reducing memorization overall may limit learning. One can understand only what one can remember (try the opposite and tell me how it works for you). To use a process of reasoning, we must remember the process. Even devising something new, we reconfigure alternatives our recall supplies. We rarely tell a student to stop remembering so he can understand better, but instead affirm each process: "Glad you got that piece [remembering]. Now let's fill in the spaces around it [understanding]." Our beachhead in the student's brain may be a few small pieces first remembered. Fleshing out the relations between them, we generate understanding. Then we return to remembering to save the whole well-understood piece.

The two processes occur inadequately under current instruction. When registering a piece for a test is the object and students know only that an answer is correct but not why, test results are only imitation learning. But while learning may limp because an answer is too narrow, it's weak also if teachers do not insist students hold onto it. Understanding left to survive by chance is more quickly and needlessly forgotten. Students soon lose even significant insights unless they nurture them, yet typical instruction conditions them to lay aside (i.e., extinguish) the prior lesson so their mind is clear for today's. A stimulating class discussion today may just displace yesterday's. Because discarding learning as fast as it arrives is so pervasive, the decision to learn permanently swims upstream against multiple impediments.

12

How You Can Help Students Assimilate Knowledge

To expand their mastery, students understand and chunk their knowledge into handy pieces they write down. They pair up and explain the pieces back to the beginning of the course, eventually facing every other student in their class. Engaging with different peers at this alters the scenario steadily in their mind, constantly leaving behind a residue of human meaning. They make answers more comprehensive by adding to them, and more permanent by re-asking the questions periodically before they forget the answers. This is not complicated.

Some teachers try to meet this need by reviewing. They read that retention depends on repeated or distributed learning, but not quite grasping cause and effect, they deliver the same material again and again, often boring students. The latter instead need to call up the knowledge from their own memory and re-explain it just like teachers do, exerting their personal effort and not just listening to others.

They need the deeper activity—like a man stumbling out of a desert into a remote truck stop and telling the clerk, "I need water," but the clerk looks him over and points him to the showers.

"I can barely stand up," the man replies hoarsely. "I need water to drink." For education to hold, working memory must assimilate ideas by its internal process rather than sloughing them off as fast as they arrive.

"We can only start students off," you may be tempted to answer. "If they want to continue their learning, it must come from them." You blame them or their milieu for their apparent lack of interest.

But the fact is we adults have twelve years of minute-by-minute control over them to work with. And in that time we still can't generate their habit of retaining knowledge? How many more years do we need? Since we don't try, more years would not matter. Our education system does not even contemplate doing this, and the understanding of how to go about it is apparently too sparsely distributed anyway.

It's not all that difficult. It just involves, first, the competent absorption of stable knowledge followed by an open-ended opportunity for each child to express it with good feelings, which provides them a motive to do it more. This happens spontaneously in real-world settings like apprenticeships that use knowledge directly. But our design of education instead removes learning from its real-world base and confines it to the artificial setting of the classroom, structured to be society's matrix where learning of all kinds is welcomed, developed, and transmitted.

The aim is admirable because skills presume a setting. Skiing? Ski slopes. Football? A gridiron, rules. Law? Courtroom, precedents. While discussion about skiing, football, or law can occur anywhere, their natural setting sustains their meaning.

We can appreciate the influence of a setting by what happens to knowledge apart from it. Think of an Eskimo, back home a respected master at surviving in the cold, when he shows up on a Hawaiian beach. Outside his home setting, his application and development of skill gradually dissipate.

A similar fate happens to the knowledge students absorb in their classroom when they carry it into alternate settings that discount it—into their social whirl, sports, and entertainment. Left untended in those venues it steadily dissolves.

If schools do not find a way to enable students to talk about their learning, they actually hinder it. Schools are not a neutral impact because they swallow up the central hours of a student's life. Failing at the role they claim as theirs, they kill students' time so that students must wait to discover for themselves a real-world setting that brings together the mental tools, topics, and peers who possess parallel knowledge. Instead of fulfilling this role, schools too often seek the mediocre purpose of installing arbitrary details that may show up on tests.

During the current months, we observe adults who aspire to lead our nation publicly discounting the value of objective knowledge. Chances are that these—who for now comprise our "best and brightest"—passed through US education. Year by year they learned and forgot, and their education became a series of checkpoints demonstrating their compliance with expectations. Mastering inclusive, objective knowledge about the world was never posed to them as a supreme value.

Figure 12.1. Once having rich recall of a subject, students' ability to think about it is a reward for their effort.

Jessica Sanders

13

How Teachers May Handle Levels of Ability

The one-room schoolhouse—one teacher, one room—helped civilize our nation. It taught all grades, all ages, and all abilities. We might guess how it did this.

1. A sense of order and mutual respect must have been essential for binding the class together. Today, developing positive attitudes and solving interpersonal problems would be particularly important. For ways to achieve this quickly, see the three books listed as references further on.
2. Students who could read on their own must have gathered much more information by themselves and summarized it in their own words, reading and writing for hours daily.
3. Teachers must have relied on better (or older) students helping the less adept (or younger). From what we know about learning a subject by teaching it, this stimulates even the better students' progress.
4. Multiple abilities in a classroom suggest rethinking school rules based on grade levels. Our system of grades is an arbitrary designation that deserves to be arbitrarily waived when it hinders sensible adaptations. In a round hole/square peg situation, obsolete rules portend failure.

5. The teacher of a one-room schoolhouse must constantly adapt even without checkpoints assigned from outside the classroom. For someone capable of handling such a situation, others should support them and remove unnecessary hindrances.
6. The approach described here offers a means of unifying instruction somewhat among differing abilities. Many teachers assume that below-average students retain most learning poorly while top students retain most learning well—in both cases the same knowledge. But quantity can mark the difference. All can master a chunk while top students do a larger one.

As students write out what they will learn, we can distinguish between full, median, and minimum answers. Students write and master what they can. You do not set them up to fail by insisting that they absorb the greater quantity that another student accommodates easily.

A rule of thumb for pacing learning is to teach what students can competently explain in impromptu and public performances. You time their learning to their ability to master it cumulatively and demonstrate it. This presumes you carry through the entire process from first understanding to final mastery for each lesson and every student.

14

What It Means to Learn a Whole Subject

Understanding one thing well, we often draw on it to understand something else. We know, for instance, the inner state of a teacher who has learned a subject by teaching it. He or she possesses conscious, connected, assimilated knowledge that seamlessly combines memory and reasoning and provides a matrix for adding new information.

That's what we want for students.

WHERE DO WE START?

We can assume that teachers enter their subject much like the rest of us. Call it the "pick and shovel" approach—identify key ideas, learn them one by one, and save them. Doing this thoroughly initiates a critical process. One piece of information ties naturally to another, and a field begins to form. When the teacher explains the field to someone else, it deepens and expands.

Learning that reinforces the whole differs from the piecemeal learning teachers usually present to students. In enabling another to understand, they refer internally to the most inclusive concepts about a subject that constitute a natural avenue for incorporating new details. Thinking "How can I help this person understand?" the teacher scans the material for the best entry point, refreshing the whole thing. The inner process of composing an explanation deepens the teacher's assimilation while students receive only the answer that concludes it. We want students to experience the inner process of development just like teachers do.

Instead of diving into the details of a new course, we begin more productively by establishing the outer edges of the field we want to fill in. We first form a sense for the whole, like putting a fence around the garden we want to plant, a frame around the picture we will paint. Essential entry points are:

What is this subject about? (the structure of the cosmos, measuring things with numbers, describing ideas in words)
What is it for? Why would people learn this? (communicate with each other, be able to manage the physical environment, stay healthy)
Who uses this knowledge? (scientists, historians, writers, doctors)
What is used in this subject? (words, numbers, pictures, physical substances)
When is this subject particularly important? (when measuring, designing, explaining, understanding)
How did this come into being? (the circumstances and needs that propelled its development)

Six points orient us to the whole, comprising an elementary tool set for grasping the subject, and helping us assign details to a structurally sound location. The points are not hard to grasp, but if we don't know them the subject remains obscure to us. Once knowing them, how could students begin to learn the subject in a way that enhances the whole while delivering the part?

A simple way is to learn first the elementary structure experts have settled upon for that field. Your current text is a source. Open it to the table of contents. Generations of thought about the subject have resulted in the design the author adopts, which is as good a beginning as any.

Let us say you have forty chapters separated into four parts. If in one hour on the first day you teach the six orienting points (so students can explain them to each other), how about in the second hour the next day students learn the four parts of the book perfectly? In two hours over two days, students grasp the foundation of a subject by mastering its orienting factors and its most elemental parts.

But say then that you continue that pace on following days, reinforcing the explanation of the global factors while adding details to the segments already learned. On the third day you might add five chapter titles—what each chapter comprises, why it is located where it is, and how it relates to the global factors. Adding just five well-understood points of knowledge per day, in a couple weeks students know a detailed summary of the entire course.

For the teacher presenting a subject, such integrative thinking occurs somewhat spontaneously because the teacher presumes context, how things are structured, how one makes sense of them. But at a pace of assimilating and saving only five new points of knowledge per day, in 180 days students can remember, explain, account for, and organize nine hundred points of knowledge.

Teachers achieve this only if they can chew gum and walk at the same time, do the multitasking of adding a new piece while sustaining its field. Students accomplish it by means of the teachers' axiom and there is no alternative. They actually have to explain the subject to someone else again and again just like a teacher does. Students obtain a global grasp of a subject as they repeatedly tell the whole thing, beginning to end. If we only want them temporarily familiar with pieces likely to appear on an imminent test, then of course we needn't do that.

Teachers benefit from a related learning phenomenon that they seldom arrange for students. Think what happens when you already know a subject, and then read a book full of fresh details about it. New points stick spontaneously because a space in your thinking looks for them ("Ah, yes! That clarifies X and that's why Z is over here"). Just by reflecting on what you read, you notice that you expand your knowledge.

Comparably, when a student reads a book about something he already knows and learns more by reflecting on it, he regards this as a reward for the effort of reading. Learning pieces and then bringing them together in his head, he experiences accomplishment.

This outcome offers a clue for the use of time. Later learning accelerates when initial learning is solid, suggesting we aim for permanent learning from the start. With early material mastered by disciplined remembering, later material attaches to it readily and soon makes the intrinsic structure of the subject the scaffold for its retention. A student becomes able to reenter it from any direction and explain it just like a teacher does.

Figure 14.1. Counting up the points of knowledge they maintain is a valid gauge of students' learning. They take pride in their growing score.
Jessica Sanders

15

How You Can Help Students Be Creative

A prerequisite for creativity is mastering the tools of its field. Originality follows from tool competence plus a passion to push an edge, a tendency to diverge from the given. We begin with mastering tools and then add opportunity. To develop a carpenter, for instance, when children are about nine we point them to a hammer, handsaw, bucket of nails, and pile of scrap lumber, and allow them unhurried time. When they believe they can cut and hammer their way through anything, we make them competent with more tools and we have our carpenter able to create with wood.

The tool set for creative thinking is an array of ideas, but they need not all originate in school. In principle, any of children's experiences worth having are worth saving. As they sum these up in writing, they add to their tool kit for creating their life. Students must have control over their ideas, ease of movement among them, like a carpenter with hammer and saw. But ahead of ease with them, students first must have them. Ability with an idea follows possessing it in the first place—remembering it. After they have it, students can take it somewhere.

Assuming we want creative people, if we discover a student being creative, what should we do? Put differently, would you worry more about a student who does what you tell him but has no personal interest in learning or even thinking about his learning, or about a student who just gets by in most subjects but passionately wants to learn one thing?

If you believe with me that the latter is in better intellectual shape and more likely to be creative, there is an implication. Students' personal motivation is delicate. When we notice that flame spring to life, we should move everything movable to encourage it. We should not deliberately construct a system that quashes children's natural motivation in order to function.

When a child exhibits a passion to learn anything at all, we can find many ways to leverage it with material we believe he should learn. We can allow scope for any initiative students reveal, exempt them from unnecessary strictures and rules, confer on them more responsibility for their own education, and enlist them to help us run the classroom and aid others' learning.

When classroom practice does not deliver a tool set of ideas that interest and nourish students, they are left with surface thinking. With no thought-generating process of their own, they depend on others' lead and are vulnerable to manipulation. We need not wonder why they sway so often with peer influence. We don't provide them their own foundation of knowledge that can withstand it.

Do you want your students able to call up the substance of the curriculum from their own assimilation of it? If so, go for that first. Once a student can explain it without help, the most potent use of time is for him to add to it and then explain it again at expanding time intervals (the teacher's axiom). Students need to spend a substantial portion of every day doing what teachers do—retrieving the subject from the depths of their own mind and expressing it. Steadily they handle questions of increasing scope.

16

How This Approach Remedies the Learn and Lose System Dominating US Education

It reverses the system point by point.

Courses do not end. You steadily recall all students' learning from the beginning of the term and back even further if you arrange for it.

Students have an incentive to retain a body of knowledge because they are asked to produce it. The mere expectation of producing it later automatically enhances the mind's retention of it.

Figure 16.1. When they might perform their learning at the end of the day, students concentrate better all day.

Jessica Sanders

Everyone has a hard copy to practice from that they can keep permanently.

The challenge involved in testing occurs hourly as students practice explaining all their learning. More extensive tests are an opportunity for students to demonstrate their mastery.

Students integrate personal interests if they wish, adding their own topics to their bag of performable questions. Curiosity adds to the brain's ability to learn.

Students learn everything instead of just pretest review questions.

Tests are not scheduled but occur without forewarning.

No learning is labeled as final.

You steadily correct and expand students' answers.

Students are fed when they demonstrate their own mastery, not just listen to someone else's.

17

How You Can Motivate Students to Cooperate

The approach described here harnesses intrinsic drives so students comply eagerly. While more often you may have observed foot dragging, excuse making, and groans, I've watched the most discouraged, angry, recalcitrant students allowed inside a school do a 180 using these methods. They amount to applying behavioral economics to education: Find out what moves people and build around it what you want.

To use this principle, get a grip first on what captures students' interest, what plows into their mind and hangs there. From their activities hour by hour, what preoccupies them? A hint is the expression on their face. They are grinning ear to ear. Another hint is their peers smiling and applauding.

You get those cues most when they nail feats in sports, entertainment, and video games. A performance ethic permeates society. Students' models and their own experience tell them that what others will watch them do is important. They value the day's lesson as they explain it to someone else because they are wired to believe that face-to-face communication is significant.

To arrange this, we define new information by the specific steps (or points, parts, references, clarifications, or associations) enabling them to comprehend it. They write it down so they are clear on what it is, and they explain it to each other so that in time the entire class monitors each one's grasp of everything taught. In this way, communication about learning becomes an avenue for relationships.

They are proud to demonstrate their competence even more as they do it formally. Significance rises with the size of the audience—from one listener to twenty or more as you end each day with an impromptu performance. A game-like flow appeals to them, so you randomize the details you can. In a bag or box place a slip containing every new question they learn, eventually incorporating an entire semester's material. Write each one's name on a Popsicle stick or chip for a separate cup.

Five minutes before the end of the day, announce, "Performance time!" As students put away their work, draw a question randomly, pause for everyone to think about it, and draw a name. The student stands, answers the question, receives applause, and you pick a new question and name. A few minutes later they leave with a palpable sense of success and mutual support.

A caveat is that performing can embarrass less knowledgeable students. One teacher noted his pupils would rather have a sharp stick in the eye than stand up and perform anything. You forestall that problem and guarantee success by defining all answers in writing, and arranging students' one-to-one practice of them before performing them to the class. Without this, performances reinforce the brighter students while adding to the others' feeling of not being quite good enough.

Several dynamics contribute to the impact of impromptu performance on students. As in sports, they practice to get better, they work as a team, an audience applauds their demonstration of skill, and they own the substance of their activity because of the effort they expended. But more fundamentally, an internal switch is thrown, a change from activity to effort.

Activity is easy to arrange because it is only students' reaction to a teacher's direction and says nothing about their inner state. Effort on the other hand issues from an internal force, an attitude, a guiding idea in a student's mind. Saying, "I want to master this," they act intentionally, claiming an outcome as their own. This occurs when motives that matter to them lead to outcomes that matter. When we press them instead to do what they cannot, or require of them what reduces their motivation, we hinder progress.

Once students regard a particular skill as significant to them, they value a way to measure their increasing mastery. Scoring delivers an independent motivational charge. If you have two skills of comparable challenge but can plot progress objectively by scoring one but not the other, the first will attract them more. Being able to tell objectively how they improve at any process increases its interest, particularly as they involve others who value the scale of improvement.

Demonstrating a new level of skill is itself a powerful motivator. Something special occurs in students when they master part of a subject, display it to peers, and receive applause. Then they are the power figure. They are the teacher. They are the performer, the focus of admiring attention, and their satisfaction rises with the challenge they surmount. As they explain a topic to different classmates, it dawns on them that, "Hey, I know this." They are pleased, and reinforce their motivation by their self-talk. Scoring their mastery of a field they say eagerly, "I'm getting better at this."

This score-able development of competence matters to students because they intuitively know that mastery of details distinguishes practitioners of any skill. The better you are, the more you show it by the range of details you routinely command. The excitement they experience in video games depends on this. The expert gamer can do what another cannot—and shows it by the score he achieves—even though the subject's value is completely arbitrary, lacking any social utility and depending only on gamers' agreement of its worth.

If challenge, scoring, accumulated skill, and comparison with others can make something that lacks any intrinsic meaning appear so valuable, surely we can accomplish the same with subject areas that affect human existence. If we can score their accumulation of knowledge in a way that correlates with their effort and their ability to demonstrate it to others, we vault them quickly onto a motivational track. Common school tests and grades fail at this for reasons of immediacy, objectivity, replicability, demonstrability, and an indirect connection between effort and results.

18

How to Include Parents

Few parents enjoy shepherding their children's homework, but with the suggestions above, students have already done the hard part of installing new learning at school. At home they can enjoy the results by showing them off. When parents are not available, it

Figure 18.1. To help students value their learning, arrange for them to explain it to more people.
Jessica Sanders

is worth a teacher's time to search out a listener for each child—a sibling, neighbor, grandparent, or teacher's aide.

Using a matching bag at home, an adult listener draws the questions, hears the answers, and applauds—a role no more complicated than that. If they want to talk about the questions ("Why . . .? How . . . ?"), students are primed to be active. They confidently expressed details they knew, offering leads for further conversation.

Parents can also help organize and maintain the notebooks containing children's hard copy of their learning, and partner with them in experiences outside school that they can add to their repertoire of knowledge in school.

19

How Students Can Perform Publicly

Performers receive what some regard as the highest reward society has to offer—the esteem of peers. It motivates performers to continue demonstrating and improving their skills. We would like students similarly motivated about their studies, so how do we go about it?

Before setting up public performances, we need to solve two problems. One is selecting performable content worth learning thoroughly, and the other is how to include all students.

On the first point we have examples like a spelling bee and math facts. These topics are handy for performance because they have clear answers students can learn perfectly and perform crisply. At first glance, however, the rest of the curriculum appears more soft-edged. Any given idea segues into a half dozen others. So how could we mark out a complete answer yet hold it within performable scope?

On the second point, top students typically elicit admiration whenever they turn around, but we need a comparable impact on the average or below-average student about their growing competence.

We solve both problems by chunking learning into demonstrable pieces. When a teacher makes a presentation and writes summary notes on the board, students might take six minutes to copy out a page of them that they later explain to a partner in one minute. Repeating this hour by hour, students master and save up capsules of learning that have a clear boundary. They demonstrate each capsule in impromptu performance in the classroom and receive applause, so a cascade of clues assures them they can deliver the material confidently.

To prepare for public performance, they assemble mastered material into larger units suitable for presentation, combining brief answers into section- and chapter-level explanations that include all their learning. For a performance they might choose a couple dozen substantial questions they can answer (minimizing overlap of topics between students), and place them in a personal bag.

On a scheduled evening, family and friends arrive as audience. Students' names are drawn randomly one at a time. The student proceeds to the front of the room and hands their bag to a moderator. Someone draws a question from the bag, skipping questions already answered. The student explains the answer and continues with other questions for their allotted time of, say, four or five minutes each, and sits down to applause. Parents serve refreshments and students mingle with adults.

20

How to Meet Required Testing

Monitoring students' progress is easy if you first ensure they understand and then write out their knowledge. If the material is left without boundaries, neither you nor they can tell whether their comprehension is complete. When everyone has a written

Figure 20.1. Students deserve a chance to show off everything they know. The opportunity to explain is a strong motivator to remember and understand.
Jessica Sanders

model in hand, you can determine whether they know it and pounce quickly on lapses ("You left out point four"). Because they explain their learning to their peers daily while you cruise about and listen, you know each one's grasp of the material. Sitting within hearing distance of four student pairs or groups, you can monitor everyone's progress, reducing the need for formative testing because you know directly the gaps to fill.

As they master required material this way, students learn everything needed and max out tests. Stakeholders soon notice that students are on track to mastery, making it easier to rely less on tests. This is a goal worth pursuing because high-stakes testing now is the final straw driving many teachers out of the profession and unnecessarily stressing students. Alternatives to an annual high-stakes test for every child are sampling, stealth measurement, multiple measures afforded by the presence of big data, inclusion of social-emotional material, and reliance on existing NAEP (National Assessment of Educational Progress) and PISA (Programme for International Student Assessment) tests.

21

How to Test Exactly What Students Know

When we test the water in a dam, the water in our test tube is incidental. What matters is the water left in the dam. The two are connected because the test-tube water should reveal that the water in the dam is pure. Tests reveal the quality of something larger, so that tests of classroom learning should accurately reflect a broader array of knowledge not tested.

We have to ask whether current testing reveals the quality of students' knowledge. The prevalence of the Learn and Lose System tells us that US education values students appearing knowledgeable, rather than being knowledgeable. The water in the education test tube often does not match the water left in the dam. Sometimes the water tested is all there is and it doesn't represent anything else at all.

And paradoxically teachers frequently observe that they teach much good material that is never tested or may find in required tests ideas students were never presented. These features diminish validity and discourage everyone. And when students can cope with tests by guessing, cramming, and review questions, the results are further suspect.

Tests furthermore may not distinguish between temporary and permanent knowledge. To align with our desire for an educated citizenry, tests should inform us of knowledge that is stable or on track to become so.

The approach offered here suggests how to tell the quality of students' knowledge. If on the one hand you say to students, "Thursday we have a test on . . . ," and then review the subject with them, tell them to read specific pages, direct them to obtain parental help, refer them to test preparation services, or allow them to review sample questions, you ensure that the test reflects passing knowledge they just acquired and will probably forget just as quickly.

That US education everywhere schedules tests ahead of time flags its intent to make students look smarter than they are. The more we massage the material and the test situation to help students show up favorably, the less believable are their scores, while tests administered without warning draw on stable, assimilated knowledge.

To resolve this problem another way, the most valid assessment is to produce their entire learning rather than a sample of it.

List on the board all the subjects your students have studied in the last two years. They sit down with plenty of blank paper and sharp pencils with erasers. One effort shows what they retain: Write out all you know about these subjects, one at a time. Tell them they have all day, and the next if needed. What they produce will be a concrete record of their true knowledge, a valid baseline.

To score it objectively, have them exchange papers. Together go through each one's paper. Identify and argue out the number of points of knowledge it contains according to the rule *Did this point require effort to learn*? Each part of a whole is a point of effort, and each step of a process or phase of a sequence. Every place the narrative could go wrong but does not indicates learning present. Whenever you test this way, apply the same criteria as before.

Once you have a baseline score for each student, tell them that periodically you will pick a section from their studies and without forewarning ask them to summarize it in writing. To master such tests, all they need to do is save what they have already learned instead of dropping it.

How you teach figures into their success. Notice how you present new material.

"Will they forget most of this?" you ask yourself. If you answer yes, you might reconsider.

"Maybe I should try a different approach." To help them learn and then go to the trouble of scoring what they are almost sure to forget is, on the face of it, a waste of time with malice aforethought.

After a few weeks of teaching for permanent assimilation, two data sets are available. One is their baseline report before they began new learning, and the other, what they can produce later by the same guidelines. Compare the two for quantity and quality, assign an objective score to each, and calculate their percent of improvement individually and collectively. Celebrate group gains.

22

+

How Testing Can Energize Students

When you labor for a year at something, how do you feel when others ignore your actual work but give you a perfunctory, "Good job," or say nothing at all? If your work itself is not worth their attention, do you feel a piece missing? What you expect is to demonstrate it to others and receive their thoughtful appreciation.

To provide this for students, you need volunteers before whom your students can do their orals in June, people who will give students the attention their year's work deserves, and describe it on a certificate they can frame and nail to their bedroom wall.

The learning that students communicate in words, in fact, lends itself to the objective measurement of time spent talking. If you can talk about something for an hour, you likely know more about it than talking about it for fifteen minutes. The measure is rough in one way but has a refined motivational impact. Students know simply to go for more, and that explaining more demonstrates their increasing competence with greater knowledge. The measure provides students a track for their effort and validly marks their growing mastery. Expanding their explanation from one minute to five to forty-five means they have actually increased their competence by that much.

A reasonable aim is for students to add one minute of new learning per classroom hour—a whole hour of effort just to tuck away a one-minute summary of it—but notice what happens then. If they master only five minutes of new material per day and retain it as I have described, do the math: 180 days times five minutes a day = nine hundred minutes = fifteen hours. In a school year they accumulate fifteen hours' worth. Picture your fifth grader in June able to answer questions for two days without repeating herself.

But let us say a less energetic student saves only a half-minute of learning per hour. He ends the year with seven and a half hours of mastered learning, still a stunning gain. And even adding only fifteen seconds of learning per hour he gains almost four hours in the school year, still more than most students can claim. When students accumulate any knowledge at a consistent pace, it adds up quickly.

Figure 22.1. Every year a student's library of what they have mastered and saved should get bigger.
Jessica Sanders

Think what you are looking for. You want to see students express a mastered chunk of knowledge proudly. As a parallel, imagine yourself as a college administrator hiring an instructor. Would you give him a three-hundred-item multiple-choice, true-false test or would you visit his current class and watch how he delivers knowledge to students? How he expresses learning in real time today tells you what he will do in your school tomorrow.

It's the same with students. We have to watch them express the knowledge that is our goal for them. If we want their enthusiastic involvement in thinking through and explaining comprehensive knowledge, that is what we must watch them do. Only performing it in front of us assures us of what they achieve.

23

How Quickly You Can Make These Changes

We explain above how using classroom time differently can increase learning. So if you understand what to do, how about starting tomorrow? There is little risk. By the end of the week your eyes and ears will tell you the outcome. In a month, you will have enough new learning for a public performance.

Relying on your direct observation of how children are moved may lead you to challenge the mass-scale changes sought these days. Think about your own relationship to such initiatives. Isn't it true that when your school insists on implementing a change, the first week you try it you can tell if it works? You can see whether it seizes students' energy and they assimilate new material. If you have to wait five years to find out whether your school's new method works, your levers have slipped way off their fulcrum.

24

What We Can Expect of Common Core

As it stands, Common Core doubles down on a flaw in US education. The flaw is the idea that students will learn material to the level of testable familiarity, then set it aside and go on to something else. That was the basic error of progressive education that has burdened instruction for almost a century. We may *hope* students retain their learning, but do not arrange their effort to ensure it.

We can contrast that error with insisting students accumulate knowledge in an ever-growing mental field. A wakeup call about this was the recent republication of a 1912 eighth grade examination that most adults today would fail badly.[1] Eighth graders then knew more than college graduates today because they were required to learn in depth and then hold onto it. Observing today's education establishment resolutely ignoring the implications of this test is understandable; it is unsettling and embarrassing to face how much the policies applied in the last hundred years have damaged learning.

In view of the temptation to blame teachers for everything going wrong, we find the basic flaw does not lie at the level of their choices. While a great many give their best effort daily to work within whatever conditions they face, the options they are handed are essentially structural and do not ensure that students accumulate knowledge.

The outcome we should ask of them is each child's mastery of their academic learning, a field formed when students can narrate, discuss, explain, and answer to their knowledge; when they do not dismiss it but keep it fresh and alive as they add to it month by month and year by year. As teachers apply this thread of Common Core, we can look forward to progress. But we cannot expect to orient learning toward this goal and simultaneously toward temporary familiarity.

Figure 24.1. Common Core will work if students save what they labor to learn.
Jessica Sanders

Eventually the public will want long-term learning from the Common Core effort, though short-term test-passing may suffice for a while. If achievement does not tick markedly upward in a few years, there will come a head-slap moment: "We've done it again. We put pressure on ourselves in yet another way and it didn't work."

We can resume progress by teaching Common Core materials (and all the other subjects not included in them) so students learn and save rather than learn and lose. All other gains grow from that seed. We have invested much cost and effort to develop levers for change. But if we don't understand how a lever works, it remains just a stick.

NOTES

1. "1912 eighth-grade exam stumps 21st century test-takers," Cavan Sieczkowski, *Huffington Post*, August 12, 2013.

CPSIA information can be obtained at www.ICGtesting.com
Printed in the USA
BVOW08s0613220815

414550BV00001B/2/P

9 781475 820669